Hypatia at the Museum

New Women's Voices Series, No. 154

poems by

M.G. Leibowitz

Finishing Line Press
Georgetown, Kentucky

Hypatia at the Museum

New Women's Voices Series, No. 154

Copyright © 2020 by M.G. Leibowitz
ISBN 978-1-64662-329-7 First Edition
All rights reserved under International and Pan-American Copyright Conventions. No part of this book may be reproduced in any manner whatsoever without written permission from the publisher, except in the case of brief quotations embodied in critical articles and reviews.

ACKNOWLEDGMENTS

Acknowledgement goes to the magazines in which these poems first appeared (sometimes in different versions):

Crab Creek Review: "The doctor puts something inside of me"
The Greensboro Review: "Schaechter's *Birth of Eve*"
Foundry: "Gentileschi's *Judith Slaying Holofernes*"
Mslexia: "Pink"
The Poetry Society: "Millais' *Return of the Dove*"
West Branch: "Women on the Peat Moor" and "The World"

Publisher: Leah Huete de Maines
Editor: Christen Kincaid
Cover Art: silavsale/Shutterstock.com
Author Photo: Conner Crutcher
Cover Design: Elizabeth Maines McCleavy

Order online: www.finishinglinepress.com
also available on amazon.com

Author inquiries and mail orders:
Finishing Line Press
P. O. Box 1626
Georgetown, Kentucky 40324
U. S. A.

Table of Contents

Unio Mystica 1

Sovereignty 2

Pentimento 4

The World 5

Raccoons, Mating 6

Pink 7

Photographing Ophelia 8

In the Prepatent Period 10

The Doctor Puts Something Inside Me 12

Web 13

Hypatia at the Museum 14

Gentileschi's *Judith Slaying Holofernes* 15

Millais' *Return of the Dove* 16

Dolphins 18

Allegory of Faith 19

Women on the Peat Moor 20

Birth of Eve 21

For my teachers

Unio Mystica

It started with the paintings:
St. Catherine of Alexandria, Magdalena penitente, Apollonia—
I laid them out on my dorm room carpet,
those of the milk bodies, all those of the downcast eyes.

St. Catherine of Alexandria, Magdalena penitente, Apollonia—
they came to me in a toothless dream,
and I cried milk as they kissed my body down.
It was a mess, of course: got in

their toothless mouths, my hair, all the dream's crevices.
O' Glorious Apollonia, patron saint of dentistry—
Of course it was a mess,
all that amateur worship. Candles forgotten,

incense left burning. *O' Glorious Apollonia, patron saint*
of pink obligation. Teach me
how to worship without candles. I'm an amateur,
sure, but I can get better at this.

Teach me what to do with these pink obligations.
I laid them out on my dorm room carpet,
then I prayed to get better.
That was how it all started, you know. With the paintings.

Sovereignty

Early spring
        and everyone is in
the orange grove
        except Mary
of course
        who is home

in Nazareth
        spinning
a yarn
        while in the grove
flowers flare
        underfoot

and the graces dance
        circling as they do
pleasure
        chastity
beauty
        and the fecundity

that overwhelms them all
        the force
of the promise
        not the thing itself
but the golden idea
        that arrow

of will
        which will not pause
for you
        relentless as it is
the motion
        prescripted

    to her bow
           like the graceful sag
  of an old house
        ceded
to the mold
        those slick

black spores
         that never seem to rest
but beget
        themselves
 mercilessly
        spore producing

spore
       which germinate
until the damp body
       surrenders
 in one terrible
       bloom

Pentimento
    After Picasso's Woman Ironing

You asked and so I posed like this:
peak-backed and craggy,

iron dumb in my hand.
Yes, I read that article in the *Times*—
the man revealed beneath me

"fleshy red tones," they said, "and
a bright red cravat."
But me, you left a scratch of gray

in a world of gray. A few strokes
on a used canvas.

I never did learn what I was meant to be ironing.
A blouson? A tablecloth?
A heavy silk skirt?

The World

When you showed it to Julian it was a little thing and perfectly round, the size of a hazelnut. *All that is made.* And I'm not saying she's a liar, but confinement does funny things to people's minds, like the Canadian grad student who saw nothing but eyeglasses after a week on his own, the aspherics mounting the bifocals as the rimless frames jeered.

Now I was walking in the belly of the city when you showed it to me: A little thing, still, no larger than a cashew and shaped just the same. It was sticky and quivering and I could just make out the shape of things churned up inside: a bicycle, five mourners, sixteen beached whales. Like all of existence was the black in the back of your throat, coughed up.

Once, while I was at a theme park as a child, a stranger pushed something wet into my hand. I held it for a moment before realizing what it was—a tissue filled with someone else's mucus. Feeling persecuted, I dropped it. "I'm sorry about that," said the nurse, as the stranger clapped his hands and smiled. "It's a gift to him, see, he thinks he's given you a gift."

Raccoons, Mating

What a silly thing this is
they seem to say, shuffling around
to keep their balance—
the male's chin resting on the female's shoulder
while she looks straight ahead—
and I wonder what it is
that keeps us rubbing up against each other when pleasure is absent,
and if Nature or Evolution could not better be explained
by saying that in sex we are reduced
to our simplest terms:
I—we say, *I*—this industrious body,
and perhaps the racoons are the same in this way, doing the thing
to know themselves raccoons, that is,
mating ridiculously in the nighttime.

Pink

It is slower than you thought
it would be: the knife balanced on the tip
of the breastbone, the movement from left
to right, the carefulness of it all—
the boy hunched over the pig as though
learning to write for the first time,
squinting over the curve of a 'c'
to make his letter match the teacher's print.
Then he wipes his forehead with an arm
and you can see the pig's grin—
her throat cavelike and fluid;
feet thrusting; no sound.
So this is what it is
to kill a thing, you think.
You had thought the sow would smell
in death, but she doesn't,
not from where you stand.
Really, it is like watching a film
in very high resolution,
even when they stick the hose
in and turn on the water,
so her head bobs with the pressure
and the water turns red.
Soon they will finish bleeding the pig,
and you will stand back
as the boys work:
hands opening the sow's belly,
carrying off her gut, her spleen.
When you ask if you can touch
something, they will give you
her skin. You'll drape it over the fence
where it hangs
like a robe,
like the pink mantle
a king might have worn
to greet his subjects
in the fields, nodding
to the dairy cow, the mountain,
the bull.

Photographing Ophelia
> *Italicized phrases have been gleaned from commentary on Ophelia by Shakespeare, Dali, Flickr comments, and others.*[1]

After all that, she says, *I'm not feeling
brave enough* to drown alone so we change
course, head to the *local swimming pool*
(deep blue water and the
electric smell of chlorine
fumes turned to chloramines), where I thank
god for the chill that's left the place
half-empty.
It's a bit modern, I know, to do this
in public, but *the river was brown*. I
just don't want to
know what was in the water—that's why I agreed when she said,
let's skip the *weedy ditch*, the *muddy death*.
Maybe go with flowers, instead, channel
Millais or something. I could have sworn these were
newly cut when I bought them but look—they've
opened too much and the petals won't stay
put. She wanted them bright and
queer, but she'll just have to settle for red and a bit
run down. We'll weave them into
some kind of crown and she can wear them while the lifeguards
take pictures on their phones. What was that? Will
they know to save her if she slipped
under? Trust me, no one could think that was part of the
venture, and anyway, we can't let her drown—
We haven't gotten the shot yet.
We need *the most desirable and frightening
woman that exists* and she looks practically

---

[1] In order, the sources include: Elizabeth Hunt, Flickr user; Rosie Hardy, Flickr user; Elizabeth Hunt, Flickr user; Rosie Hardy, Flickr user; *Athenaeum* reviewer of John Everett Millais' *Ophelia* as cited in Andrew Scull's Madness: A Very Short Introduction; Gertrude's description of Ophelia's death in Hamlet; Salvador Dalí on Millais' *Ophelia*

xanthippic floating there in the water. Try not frowning, dear.
Yes! Like that. Think of nothing, let your mind grow moss.
You know, I'm starting to doubt the whole thing, now, like maybe we zeroed in on wrong the scene in the play.

In the Prepatent Period

I told myself it was
an impermanence,
deed

but I saw the years
stretched fibrous
in the sun.

It was not
unlike a recluse's web:
full of silent presence.

As a girl,
I was bitten.
My fault. Playing

in the garage
where I was not
supposed to go.

I felt little when it bit:
a mild stinging,
a sheen of yellow

pain,
but I saw the creature
as it left me,

practically running
down my calf.
I told myself

there was little to do.
It was early
to know for sure.

There was nothing
to do but go home,
keep an eye on it.

Nothing to do
right now
but wait.

The Doctor Puts Something Inside Me

so I will not bleed anymore. I say thanks,
hand twenty dollars to the receptionist
on my way out. Lately, I've been feeling squeamish
about the insides of things. The wet yolk too yellow,
globoid, like a mole on an oiled back.
I don't bleed anymore, but I see faces on everything:
a hummingbird; the nail heads staring from my bookcase—
lately, my body's been asking for things
I don't want. Hand slipping under my shirt
while I wait at the bus stop. Fingers on the swell
between waistband and navel. It will be April soon.
Mildew will flourish between bathroom ceiling tiles,
and the hummingbirds will return to build small homes.
Outside my window, the caterpillars
are starting to fall. I see them everywhere: black Tussocks
with hairy backs, digressive bodies—
I don't know how they know when it's time to start molting.
Skin stretched and breaking over widening frames.
Then the setae cocoons on the undersides of eaves.
And the moths inside, the females' stunted wings.

Web

After Nina Katchadourian's Mended Spiderweb *series*

In Pörtö, a woman mends a spider web.
Red threads, white glue. *It's a gift*, she says.
I'm giving you a gift.

Arachne displeased. Arachne raging.
In the morning: Red threads dumped
on the grass. Tiny, silken stitches

make the web whole.

Hypatia at the Museum

In the painting of St. Catherine that hangs
        in the Uffizi, you are the white and pink

of a mammalian belly, standing calmly
        before the fire and the wheel.

A moment ago, your robe slipped
        from your shoulders. Now you cover

yourself with your hands, consider something
        beyond the painting's frame.

Strange, the distance between some bodies
        and minds. You seem not to notice the hands

that clutch at modesty,
        the body and its snorting, grousing,

rooting towards the warmth. Weak body,
        with its wants and its wills—

What shameful things,
        the appetites.

I hold mine close.
        Warm, wrinkled

things that flutter
        by my legs.

Moths breathing
        under the sheets.

Gentileschi's *Judith Slaying Holofernes*

He
[me]   on   the edge of the bed

          pushing   with a hand
          to prevent
[him]
              Lifting
         his face
I   pulled his hair   tight
and
         with [a] knife
             removed a piece of flesh
It is true
it is true
it is true
it is true

I   have killed him
           best I could

Words, other than those bracketed, are excerpted from Artemisia Gentileschi's courtroom testimony against her rapist as found in Mary D. Garrard's Artemisia Gentileschi: The Image of the Female Hero in Italian Baroque Art.

Millais' *Return of the Dove*

I
and the girls have been floating
in this barn
for almost a year

remembering and forgetting
the simplest things

the white rocks of home soil
the water sitting meekly
in ponds

the way sunlight streamed
shiftingly
in a million shades

not like urine
in a single
yellow cord

II
a year is not enough
to lose the word for *green*
but it's more than enough time to misplace
the smell of it

how it rose to greet them
in the early morning
yeasty and sweet

the summer grass
carrying it forward
carrying it forward

III
while at sea
no one breeds

not the lion
the moss crab
the ostrich
the bee

even the sons
don't dare touch them

IV
then the dove—

slipping in
through the window
godly
little heartbeat
more motion than sound

V
and you imagine the girls
not rejoicing
but kissing the dove
with kisses of obligation

as they consider its neck

how feeble it is
just a handful of feathers

how simple it would be
how quick

Dolphins

In half an hour, we'll be standing
               under the public showers and I'll see
shit on your thighs.
             I'll say nothing. For now, we hold hands
me, my father, you
             and crawl through the ocean,
everyone's bowels holding up,
             our faces below water. We hear them first,
those whinnying clicks that seem to sound
             from all around. Then they come, one
after another, after another.
             Quick as years, they slide beneath
us, those strange, adipose bodies
             slapping against your skin.
Making you shiver.
             They aren't exactly beautiful, you tell me later,
but did you see how they moved? In the water,
             we are tied into masks and goggles,
looped into plastic fins.
             And then there's you, 82,
stopping every few yards to rest
             like an infant in my father's arms.

Allegory of Faith
    After Vermeer's Allegory of the Catholic Faith

"She looks like a fish," a woman says,
and it's true: pose of a mackerel

hooked and hauled from sea, wide-set eyes
staring stupidly at the sky. And you wonder how Vermeer

got her to pose like that: one hand clutching her breast,
one leg balanced improbably on a globe.

Faith herself appears uncomfortable.
How many minutes did it take for her feet

to grow numb, for her supporting arm to ache?
Maybe she brought the apple to snack on;

tucked it in the flounces of those sleeves
and snuck tiny bites whenever he looked down.

It would have been warm in the room,
heat trapped by the tapestry and stone.

I bet the apple slipped from her sweating palms,
rolled to the foreground. When she reached for it,

Vermeer said, "Wait!" Imagine him giddy, suddenly inspired,
sketching chalice, cornerstone, apple, snake.

Women on the Peat Moor
After Van Gogh's Women on the Peat Moor

First there were four, then only two
women braced against the sky.
The others hid themselves

darkening their bodies with midnight blue
until they dried.

It was Van der Wheel
who gave them the idea. The guy
hated clutter, any display

with too many figures.
So they simplified:
two in the field of view

bending slowly, as if they knew
the child can be soothed
by moving the red ball
behind the blue,
which they do.

Birth of Eve

Before she learned anything, eve was a fetus
in the uterus of adam's rib, a pocket of air
with red hair and eyes like supercomputers.
When she blinked, she made flowers. I asked,
do you know what you are? and she waved her
hands, the gray-blue of stone or something
too cold to touch. I tried to touch
and the fluid around us stopped breathing.
Later, I asked god if he meant
for things to end up like they did: the trees
bowed and languid in their nakedness, the people
clothed like strange birds, the world not
breathing. He told me that's the way things
work out sometimes, and I said, that's not
an answer, and he smiled and ruffled my hair
until I felt like a strange bird, like my hair
was wings—they would take me to the end
of any world.

M.G. Leibowitz was born and raised in New York. Her work has appeared in *Creative Nonfiction, Foundry, The Journal,* and *West Branch*, among others. M.G. received her BA and MA in philosophy and religious studies from Stanford University, and was the recipient of a 2019 fellowship from the Bucknell University Stadler Center for Poetry. *Hypatia at the Museum* is her first collection.

www.ingramcontent.com/pod-product-compliance
Lightning Source LLC
LaVergne TN
LVHW041522070426
835507LV00012B/1750